DESTINY

A GUIDE TO REALIZING YOUR PURPOSE

DESTINY

A GUIDE TO REALIZING YOUR PURPOSE

KEVIN N. CARPENTER

Table of Contents

Preface

The idea of writing this book came to me shortly after I was approached by the executive of the leading African American business publication. It was a cold day in February of 2022, and I was working onsite at my company's facility in Orville, Ohio when I stepped away to take the call. He informed me that I was not only selected to be one of the 2022 Most Influential Black Executives, but also one of few awardees asked to write an article that would later be featured in the edition. He said, "I can see why you are so influential. It's a shame that I hadn't recognized you earlier. Not only have you excelled at work, but your philanthropic accomplishments within the community, universities, and with people are also outstanding. You're just doing what is required and needed for equity, and that is a testament to your amazing influence."

As someone who grew up facing financial difficulties and poverty in Alabama, I was honored to have someone who barely knew me speak such kind words. I do not accept accolades and compliments very well, so I was taken aback to hear acknowledgment of the scope of my career and philanthropic endeavors all in one phone call. He asked me to write an article on how young Black business professionals can follow my career trajectory into executive positions, and I soon realized that this was a unique opportunity for me to impart some wisdom to anyone looking to accomplish something great. This was my chance to speak to those facing seemingly insurmountable obstacles and to share some encouragement from my perspective as a Black man striving and thriving in Corporate America.

After speaking with the magazine's executive, I told my boss about my feature. I wanted to get his thoughts on the matter since I would be representing our company. My boss said, "I'm not surprised that you were chosen for this award. I am honored that you work here with me and for me, and I know that you are going to make a great impact on our company. Just let me know what I need to do to support you." He could have easily told me that the company did not need this type of publicity, but he welcomed my exposure, which assured me of the fact that I truly had the company's support.

Although it was cloudy and cold in the Midwest when I received that phone call, on the inside, I was beaming with gratitude as I came to realize the full weight of my blessings. I was not only bestowed unprecedented recognition for my career, but I was also afforded the amazing opportunity to encourage aspiring leaders. Then, on top of all of that, I was working at a wonderful company that supported my accomplishments.

So, from this pivotal juncture of my life, I was inspired to write this guide to help blaze the trail for aspiring leaders in Corporate America and environments across the world. As you read this book, I hope that the concepts and stories will help you manage your fear and operate in faith as you walk in your purpose and live out your destiny.

Introduction

What comes to mind when you hear the words *destiny* and *purpose*? Have you envisioned your destiny or realized your purpose? Destiny is something to which a person is called to attain or achieve, and purpose is the reason why you exist. Everyone in God's world has a purpose and a reason for existing. Both destiny and purpose allude to an internal power compelling you to press forward, and if you've ever had a goal or project to complete, you've felt this power pushing you to get it done. As a leader, your ability to guide yourself and your people with purpose to the desired end is critical.

This guide is designed to help you strengthen your internal power by focusing on four concepts: 1) vision, 2) taking on difficult jobs, 3) understanding mental challenges, and 4) being patiently impatient. We will go over the tools needed for you to take hold of these concepts and integrate them into your life and career so that you can live a full and abundant life.

I chose to work in Corporate America because it is dear to me, and it is where I was purposed to affect the world. Each person who lives out their purpose will impact the world in some way, and if everyone impacts the world with their purpose, the world will undoubtedly become a better place.

Unfortunately, we all face challenges in Corporate America and the world at large. I would dare say that the world exists in its current state because so many people are not living out their true purpose. The disappointment that comes with not living out one's true purpose can cause a person to be angry and go against those who are purpose-driven.

We hear a lot of nonsense and negativity from famous people on social media, but the people who are truly proficient and have the knowledge to share are often ignored. So, I am sharing my insight with those who are willing to listen. So much negativity enters our eyes and ears to the point where it fills us with fear and makes us lose hope.

Create your own environment, and don't just look at what you see in front of you. Use your faith to continue moving despite roadblocks or clouds. Create an internal sunshine that continues glowing despite the external environment, spreading light to all those around you.

I may not have a lot of colorful stories to tell you, but sometimes, things are simply what they are. I don't have to jump up and down for you to know that I have the Spirit of the Lord dwelling inside me. Sometimes, I stand in silence and peace as if nothing is going on, even if there is a party happening inside me. At times, you will have to talk yourself into being happy when there is no one else to do it for you. You may have to look at the obstacle in your way and not only tell it to move, but force it to disappear.

I hope this book encourages you to stop living in fear and start walking in your purpose. I hope that you will move forward with the things that seem difficult and know that you can accomplish them with hard work. I hope that you will operate with faith and an unshakable belief in yourself and in what you can become. I hope that you truly realize what you have been put on this Earth to accomplish.

You will have dark and difficult times, but you will win if you endure what is coming against you. Be tougher than your environment. Know that in the end, you will win.

VISION

As a child, I frequently dreamt about what I would grow up to become. When I participated in my fourth-grade sweetheart contest, I was asked what I wanted to be when I grew up. My nine-year-old self said, "I want to be a doctor, and I want to help people!" Although I did not become a doctor, I have fulfilled my desire to help people. Like me, you too were probably asked as a child, "What do you want to be when you grow up?" Your answer may have seemed outrageous at the time, or even unattainable to most. Yet you still believed that you could accomplish anything you set your mind to. Then life, obstacles, and adversity happened, and that childhood vision no longer felt attainable.

Although your vision may not look like it once did, ask yourself what your current aspirations or dreams are. You must dream big, and not be overwhelmed by the magnitude of your vision. Do not stop, because the world needs you. Dreamers are needed for the world to keep moving forward.

Vision is the big, bright, immaculate goal that sits so far out of reach that it seems as though you will never get there. A vision is like a castle perched up on a hill that is admired from a great distance and has a treacherous winding path to get to it. Despite the expected obstacles along the path, people who are striving to get there will devise a plan and start on that journey toward it. Along the way, they may doubt, pause, or even turn back, but ultimately, if a person stays the course, they will get to that castle, which is the goal.

This type of vision and goal setting is crucial for leadership. As an aspiring leader, each role you take in your career is part of your journey toward the seemingly unattainable place that you envision. With such pursuits, your vision starts with an internal urging that pushes you forward. Life is hard. It will eat you up and spit you out. But strong leaders are built to take on life's challenges and not give up. Our strength is derived from our tenacity to move forward. We persevere! After overcoming an obstacle, you can reflect upon it and realize that you gained strength and valuable experiences from pursuing your vision.

Envisioning does not always involve spoken words; it may start with simply visualizing yourself in the place you yearn to be. You may also draw sketches and pictures, or create vision boards related to your goals. Then, as things start to manifest, your vision becomes even more tangible.

As a child, I envisioned that I would someday work in Corporate America, ultimately becoming a CEO of a Fortune 500 company. I saw that as my life's vision. Later, as a newly minted engineer fresh out of college, I wrote, "I want to be a CEO of a Fortune 500 company" on a sticky note and placed it on my desk. It was the year 2000, and I was sitting on North River Road in Warren, Ohio, where I worked as an applications engineer for Delphi Packard Electric. That vision has persisted throughout my life and career and continues to impact each role I embrace.

Throughout my twenty-five-year-and-counting career, I've worked as an engineer, program manager, and project leader. I have worked in large companies and earned a Master's in Business Administration

(MBA), alongside other advanced degrees. I have also worked in office settings and manufacturing plants and have even spent time working overseas. I excelled at all the different roles that I took on, and eventually became proficient in various aspects of Corporate America. Each of my professional experiences were a step along the path toward my ultimate vision of being a CEO. My motivation to fulfill this vision to lead stems from my love of people, and my desire to guide them. I am called for this purpose.

Along the way, there were a lot of ups and downs. I encountered both good and bad people, and I learned from each. I encountered a lot of naysayers, tough jobs, and hard times in both my personal and professional life. I was divorced and had children, so I had to take some steps back and even stop at times. Despite it all, I still held on to that vision of becoming a CEO someday.

The journey to excel in life or corporate leadership is not easy, and you will have to build your inner confidence. Most times, you will be the only one who will believe in your dream, and you must be okay with seeing and articulating your vision when no one else can. It is your life's purpose, and you must own and be accountable for making it happen. Stay steadfast in knowing that you will realize it. You were born to do it. It is your birthright and purpose!

Having a vision for your life is akin to a mother being with child. She wants to birth that child to life. Similarly, you should also want to bring your vision to pass because you will leave the world better than you found it. Your vision is that piece of the puzzle that we are forming as a society. Each of us must capture our place in the world. If we are not in the right place, we are not adding the value that we were destined to add to this world.

As you determine the vision and purpose of your career, you should ask critical questions. What is your goal, and what steps do you need to take to accomplish it? What internal and external obstacles will you likely face? Were you born into an environment that may create an inertia that works against you? What roadblocks and systemic issues are in place? What behaviors are you exhibiting that make you your own worst enemy?

Your vision is your calling. To succeed, you should set goals. Finishing kindergarten, graduating from high school with a 4.0 grade point average (GPA), going to medical school, earning $1 billion in revenue in a business, and opening a food truck are various goals you can set. As you set goals, it is also important to have a plan for how you will accomplish them.

I was taught to be a list maker early on, so I have the habit of creating to-do lists. When you write out goals, whether on paper or digitally, you are much more likely to accomplish them. As you devise a plan, you will come up with strategies and manageable actions that will get you to your ultimate goal. If your goal is to graduate from high school with a 4.0 GPA, your strategy may be to study for two hours each night, take certain classes, and meet with your math teacher for twenty minutes after class once a week. These strategies will help you reach that goal in the end.

Additionally, once some time has passed, you will need to reflect and determine whether you succeeded at those tactics. Be truly honest with yourself. This is your say-do ratio. You may say that you will accomplish something in a certain amount of time, but were you successful? What did you learn and what mistakes did you make? Do not look at setbacks as failures; they are just temporary defeats that should push you forward. These questions will help guide your journey and set up a dashboard that gives you a pulse on your progress.

As you lead a goal-oriented and purpose-driven life, as Paulo says in *The Alchemist*, the Universe conspires to make your goals happen. Life has a way of gearing you toward your vision even before you are fully aware of it. If you live by this early in your career, great! However, it is never too late to start. Planning, setting goals, establishing tactics, and keeping score of your progress are crucial for success.

It is also important to heed guidance along the way and try to avoid life's pitfalls. One of my first memories of receiving proper guidance was when I worked with my grandfather laying bricks at the age of twelve. Along with Granddad, who was the first Black brick mason in Tuscaloosa, Alabama, I also had the pleasure of working alongside my Uncle Alan and my stepdad, Art. We were a crew of construction workers with many other guys from around town. Even though I was only twelve years old at the time, I was surrounded by a crew of grown men. Their language was very offensive, but to a twelve-year-old, it was cool.

After listening to the vulgar language, I started using it myself in my daily speech. This was not representative of what I had been taught by my grandparents, and my stepdad simply laughed at me right along with the crew every time I cursed. He did not correct my actions. I needed to be corrected, but this showed me that he was not vested in me as much as I was vested in him.

My stepdad, Art, was a great man in his own right, but he did not use this as a teachable moment to correct my actions. By the age of twelve, I had known him for about eight years, and he had never really spent time with me as a dad should. I have always spoken of the hope of what I wanted our relationship to be. I learned from that experience, and I use it as an example of how not to engage with my own children. I don't take anything away from him. I love him dearly and he is my father, but at that time, he did not fulfill the fatherly role I so desperately needed.

My Uncle Alan, however, *did* take on that fatherly role in this instance. Uncle Alan was my mother's brother and a fabulous brick mason. He was the person on the crew who said, "You know you don't talk like that." That showed me that my uncle was vested in me, and he loved me. When he saw a sign of me going in the wrong direction, he provided the slight correction I needed to get back on track.

In the pursuit of your goals, you will encounter many seemingly small choices that have the potential to become life-impacting habits. As a kid, those choices may have been taking a sip of beer, a quick smoke of a cigarette, or being a class clown. As an adult, the decision may be whether to skip that class and spend time binging your favorite television series. You will always need to make choices that are conducive to your growth. If not, vices can take over your life. Along the way, you will encounter many people who will nudge you back on track. I call them *guardrail people* because they make you aware of your faults and help you quickly correct your ways. Listen to the people who are invested in you to help you stay on the path to your destiny.

Some people help guide you, while others are simply there to observe your journey. Those observers may see your present life and assume that it has always been a certain way. They do not see the blood, sweat, tears, and sacrifices that you have made. They do not see all the things that lead to "here." Life is not social media, where we can see a highlight reel to summarize years of experiences. Often, a lot of the critical highlights of a person's life are kept hidden. Most of the downsides are intentionally not shared, as well. Not everything is meant to be shown, but some things are meant to be told to set others free and to let them know that they are not alone in their struggle. I enjoy living life to the fullest, and I share these stories not to boast, but to inspire others to live their lives to the fullest, as well.

During those downsides, always look for a glimmer of encouragement and motivation to keep moving ahead. As a high school student in Douglasville, Georgia, I had an experience where I was motivated to persist despite my circumstances. The time had come for me to drive a car to school, but my family barely had a decent car for me to drive. This was in the early 1990s, and we had a Cadillac, a 1978 Sedan Deville, and a 1978 Ford Futura that my stepdad received from his father. I was proud of the Ford Futura, which my parents let me drive, even though I had to add oil to it each time I cranked it up. I kept cases of 1-quart containers of oil in the back, and every time I started the car, I had to use that funnel to pour the oil into the engine. I would crank it up and go about my way, and it would smoke like hell, but I'd be proud.

I liked to dress nicely, so I would proudly emerge from my car looking great despite the oil and smoke. Even then, I knew that my predicament was not my end. I knew my situation at the time was not in my control, and that it would not be my final resting place. With that car, I chose to appreciate that it could get me from point A to point B, and that I could take my brother and sister to Cumberland or Green Briar Mall. I was grateful to have something to drive, but at the same time, I was patiently impatient. I was mindful that I was just passing through that circumstance. That car had duct tape on the makeshift plexiglass window, which my stepdad and I had creatively made to replace the broken glass window. My situation was something that I could have cried and moaned about. I could also have taken different directions to gain money in seedy ways. Instead, I was taught the lesson of appreciation. I wanted more, and I used my circumstances as motivation to go to school and work hard to get it.

On one occasion, I walked out of the school building and found that my friends had pranked me by decorating my entire car. Some of these guys, like

Freddie, didn't even have a car. He always liked to make jokes about people, including me, even though I picked him up for school every morning. The guys had decorated the car in newspaper and placed the funnel that I used to put oil into the car onto the antenna. As I walked towards the car with a girl, I couldn't help but shake my head and laugh. The crazy thing about it is that she looked at me and said, "I don't care; you're Kevin Carpenter." At the time, I didn't realize what that meant, but I know what it means now. She saw my light, and she knew that I was destined for greatness. Nothing else mattered.

Oftentimes, people see your light before you do. Of course, I would have liked a nice car to ride around in like many of the other kids at Lithia Springs Comprehensive High School. Of course, I got embarrassed sometimes when I drove up to the school. But even still, I held my head high and knew that it was not in my hands at that time. I promised myself that when my circumstances were finally in my control, my life would change for the better. The thing about obstacles and experiences is that you could have a cup of coffee somewhere, but you don't need to stay there and have a full-blown, four-course dinner. I was just passing through because my purpose and destiny were so much more, and I knew it.

Now, I realize that this was just a simple car, but as a seventeen-year-old boy, that was my world. I could have stayed in a funk and felt sorry for myself. But I chose to keep pushing until I was admitted to Morehouse College and Georgia Institute of Technology. I chose to excel in school and my internships because these were all things that were in my control. It was impractical for me to take my salary from Burger King and put it towards a nicer car. That car was just a steppingstone, and I used it as motivation for greater things that would eventually come my way — things that were in my control. Regardless of the circumstances, always look for the lessons because that's how you overcome it. I love that old Ford Futura. I wouldn't be where I am today without it.

The obstacles you experience as you get closer to your purpose are there to distract you. The enemy will come after you very aggressively. Be mindful because you can spend your life moving towards a goal, and then one mistake could end it all. As a child, my grandmother told me to always be aware of my surroundings to ensure my safety. Sometimes, the people that can harm you the most are those closest to you and those who are supposed to protect you. They can often be the ones that lead you into trouble.

For instance, I wanted my marriage to succeed, but it ended up being one of my biggest obstacles and failures in life. For me, marriage was always about legacy and the family unit. Purpose and destiny are all about the foundational piece of marriage, children, and breaking generational curses. Along that journey, the person that I looked to for help, kindness, and support was the one who was tripping me and making me jump through unnecessary hoops. The enemy used the one closest to me to deter me from the great purpose I was put on this Earth to fulfill. This life lesson left me with a significant pain body, which is something that holds the old emotional pain inside of a person and loves using that pain to control the person's thinking. This was a situation that was designed to kill me and stop me from realizing my true vision.

Frequently, the person closest to you sees your light up close, which can be difficult for them. If those around you are not strong, the enemy will use those folks to trip you. As you grow and experience life, be mindful of the people that you care about and choose to keep close. Obstacles come in all different shapes and sizes and come from unexpected places. I read something interesting that Bishop Bonner said; he said not to expect someone who passed on the generational curse to help you break it. Generational curses are usually passed down from parent to child and can cause huge roadblocks that must be addressed. If left unaddressed, these and other family-based obstacles can be the strongest hindrances to your success.

One pivotal situation occurred around 2001 when I had a fellowship opportunity with Delphi to attend Harvard Business School. While going through the application process, I decided not to pursue it. I made that decision for all the wrong reasons. Part of my life's dream was to go to Morehouse College and Georgia Institute of Technology, to get a master's degree in engineering, and then eventually go to Harvard Business School. These were different milestones that were to get me on the right trajectory to becoming a CEO. In my mind, those steps were imperative for me to accomplish my goal.

At that time, I decided not to go because I wanted to impress my wife. I heard her brag about a friend of ours who went to seminary school and was an accountant. She bragged that he chose God over business or Corporate America. I always knew that I could choose both because I wanted my ministry to be in corporate settings. I wanted to push the positive core values to great companies in the corporate arena. It has worked out for me thus far, but at that time, I didn't see things as clearly. I was just a man trying to please my unpleasable wife.

As you go through this journey, you must learn from your delays, temporary defeat, and bad decisions. You must get the lesson in all things, and you can never let a hiccup in your trajectory be a stop. Pause, assess the situation, and be mindful moving forward.

Now, I reflect on that time more mindfully. While going through it, I knew it was a terrible idea to halt my business school education. Shortly after, I decided not to pursue an MBA. My marriage, which was already failing, continued to unravel, and eventually ended in divorce. I thought, "Man, I wish I had not done this. I wish I had not gotten married. I wish I had not moved to Detroit. I wish I would have just followed my dream and gotten my Harvard MBA and I would have been on to fulfilling my purpose."

I thought that being married was one of the milestones. I was looking at the way the corporate guys did it and the people before me did it. The route was to get married, show stability, and then move on to get your MBA and your career path would be set. But some people go that route, and they are still not set.

What I am getting at is that it was totally up to me to recognize that it was time to stop because it was not going to work. I left Delphi and went to Magna. I was still gaining experience and taking on hard jobs, but it wasn't going according to my supposed plan in what I thought was the "right" order. Although I was still trusting the process, myself, and my faith, I was also in a state of questioning myself. All in all, I knew that there was something for me to learn from the situation.

These life changes took place from about 2001 to 2007. Despite my challenges, I worked in several different areas during that time and became a design engineering manager. I went on to become a program engineering manager, a program manager, a product manager, and a senior product manager. I went on to earn my executive MBA degree from Case Western Reserve University, which at the time was #19 in the country for executive MBA degrees. General Electric (GE) sponsored my degree while I worked there in Cleveland, Ohio. So, even when I thought I was stagnant, I was, in fact, making some major moves and gaining some of the best experiences of my career. I could have easily given up or stopped, but I continued to move and remained open so that I could learn from my experiences. I was able to turn a temporary defeat into a victory, which was part of the journey that led me to where I am today.

You must press through your obstacles and endure to gain experience and learn lessons. You will have accomplished another goal, and you will be stronger on the other side. The downside of overcoming obstacles is that those experiences often leave emotional pain inside of a person that impacts a person's thinking. You must be mindful of and address the pain. If not, it will trip you up and prevent you from pressing forward. Instead of breaking through the wall, you will keep bumping your head against it. Sit down and record those pain bodies so that you can address them. Seek counseling to learn how to deal with them effectively. If you don't, they are going to be the deciding factor and force behind why you can't get to your destined place.

It is great to have big dreams, a vision board, and goals, but you must work to make those dreams come true. Your discipline in doing the small daily tactics will be key in this case. You cannot just be a talker who says what you're going to do something with no action. This leads to a life filled with disappointment. When I talk about vision, goal setting, and strategy, they are always in the framework of execution. How will I deploy that strategy or plan? The person facing you in the mirror must answer that question. When I ask myself this question, I know that I cannot blame external factors in my lack of progress, because as part of my strategy, I must account for those factors and obstacles. I cannot blame my mother, the white man, or the Black man. If I don't achieve what I said I was going to achieve, that solely rests on *my* shoulders. I did not get it done; I did not execute.

Execution is the imperative step in bringing your vision to pass. It is the hard part, and often where we fumble. Challenges experienced during execution lead to half-assed efforts and cause us to turn back. You must define your vision, create goals, strategize, and above all else, execute.

CHALLENGING WORK

As I reflect on challenging work, my remarkable grandfather who taught me the value of hard work comes to mind. He blazed the trail and employed so many in the community. Watching him toil until late into his life was so inspiring. My first job working alongside him laying bricks in the hot Tuscaloosa sun was challenging, to say the least. I was his mortar boy, and he let me lay the occasional brick. At twelve years old, I worked five or six days a week. I remember telling him that I wanted to be just like him, and he told me to be an engineer instead because his work was very hard.

The lessons I learned in that hot sun still resonate with me today. Those lessons taught me about perseverance and teamwork, and that anything worth having is going to be challenging. That job stretched me. My body was sore, and I lost all my baby fat, but I was better on the other side.

Another early experience with challenging work started when I entered Morehouse College in 1992. I was eager to begin my studies and become an engineer.

I saw this as my first step on the road to manifesting my vision of becoming a CEO of a Fortune 500 company. When you enter college to study engineering, the goal is to be placed in no lower than Pre-Calculus II. Calculus is ideal because it allows you to get your degree and graduate on time. I was in a Mathematics and Electrical Engineering dual degree program with Morehouse College and Georgia Institute of Technology.

As a high school graduate who had not studied the last six months of my senior year, I was unprepared for the true rigor I encountered upon my arrival on campus. When I read my placement scores after the first week, I was shocked to see that I had bombed my placement test and was placed in basic math. Above all, I was embarrassed because math was the subject I loved and excelled at most. I was devastated and my ego was hit. When my classmates found out, they told me, "You need to change your major; you're never going to graduate." These were people placed in Pre-Calculus II or Calculus. Some of them even told me that

I would never make it as an engineer if I started from basic math.

I decided that I was not going to let this obstacle deter me. When I embark upon a goal, I am steadfast, and I speak with conviction. I believe in Kevin Carpenter and in what God has purposed me to become. I had the conviction to know that if I was purposed to become an engineer, then this obstacle was just a steppingstone.

As I reflect on that time now, I can say that I took every math class offered at Morehouse College. While going through this experience, I was mocked and ridiculed. I was a big talker, so that made the mocking even worse. Despite that, I spoke with conviction and said, "I will be an engineer, and I will catch you guys in math. When I catch you, I will pull you right along with me." I did not say it in a vengeful way, I meant that I would catch up with them, study with them, and succeed alongside them. I never sought revenge toward those who mocked me. We became friends and they will attest to this even today.

I could have allowed this experience to shatter my ego and shake my confidence. The conviction I spoke with could have been just a loud horn with no backing. Instead, I use that experience to remind me to live by my favorite Abraham Lincoln quote, "Prepare and get ready, and perhaps my day will come."

When I entered Morehouse, I had not prepared myself. So, what I learned as an eighteen-year-old in August of 1992 was that I am to always stay ready, so I don't have to get ready. I will always be prepared, and my day will come, but it is not going to catch me off guard as it did that day as a college freshman.

I learned the lesson, took the experience, and received a strong foundation of mathematics. I became a hell of an engineer, which is an ode to Georgia Tech's fight song. I became a hell of an executive, I will become a hell of a CEO, and most importantly, I became a hell of a person. At that point in time, perhaps I needed to get the lesson and form relationships with the people I met along the way in those math classes that folks ruled out. I needed to meet people like Marlon King, Joe Miller, Terry Lee, Darryl Londyn, and all the other amazing folks that I encountered. By being counted out, and subsequently building those lifelong relationships, I was able to get ready.

Inevitably, life will hand you challenging situations that were not of your creation, and that is when you will start to see what you are truly made of. Those unexpected circumstances will reveal your ability to find the light in the darkest of times.

Challenging work also prepares you for new opportunities. As you choose to take roles that force you to step outside of your comfort zone, an opportunity may come along that matches what you have been preparing for. That is providence. Let's look at the other end. What if you had not prepared and taken on the challenging work? What if you had remained comfortable? That would leave you unprepared and without confidence when the opportunity comes. Challenging work builds confidence, which allows you to say, "I can do this."

What did David say when Saul told him to fight Goliath? David said, "I don't need your sword or your equipment. I will use my slingshot because the bear prepared me for the lion, and the lion prepared for the uncircumcised Philistine." David exuded that confidence because he had been taking on the challenging work of protecting his sheep. That example shows that David was preparing at every step along the way, even before he realized that he was going to be king.

Sometimes, you will look at a situation or obstacle and wonder how it is propelling you toward what you are destined to be. Then, when you get to that place, you will then realize that those challenges were things you had to endure to be capable and ready to kick butt. Those experiences are the pieces of the puzzle that make your journey worth it. As you embrace that challenging work, you are becoming prepared for even greater difficulties that will come your way. There is nothing worse than having the opportunity and squandering it by being unprepared.

Pay attention to what you may gain from each opportunity. For instance, even if you are not excited about a role, taking it may be the right decision. You might need to take a step sideways in order to go up. It is easy to get excited about that big phone call that you were looking forward to, but what if you take a job and it is not what you expected? What if it was just a sidestep that would prepare you for the big job? Be ready to not only receive the great calls, but also receive the calls that are going to build your tools, skills, endurance, character, and fortitude.

Taking uncomfortable and challenging jobs that no one else wants is how you gain experience and discipline, which no one can take from you. I gained these character traits working as a cook at Burger King in high school and loading boxes while going to college. Then, early in my career, I gained more experience working at General Motors as a controls engineer during the day and a plant supervisor in the metal stamp area at night. At one point early in my corporate career, while working as an engineer by day, I worked nights selling business suits at a popular men's dress store. I wanted to understand the customer experience and have that as a tool in my toolkit. These and many other jobs prepared me to excel at my craft and took me closer to my vision of becoming a CEO of a Fortune 500 company.

Another challenging job that I experienced was when I was a Senior Design Release Engineer (DRE) for Delphi in the early 2000s. I was supporting General Motors on their biggest truck line, GMT800. They built about 1.7 million units a year—the most units of any vehicle line at that time. It had a great profit margin, and it was a flagship. Pretty much every other division ate off that line at General Motors; so, as GMT800 went, so went GM. That line had seven plants in the United States, Canada, and Mexico. I worked on the wiring harnesses, which were among the most vital parts of the vehicle.

I had to work closely with Jageer Such, who was disgruntled. Jageer had been at GM for over thirty years. His first wife, whom he loved, died, and he later remarried and divorced his second wife. So, he wasn't very happy, and no one wanted to work with Jageer. Jageer had a wealth of knowledge, and I had no choice but to work with him since I was the youngest person on this team of senior-level engineers.

Each team member had an average of twenty-eight or thirty years at the company. This was the job for either those with the most experience or those who were looking to gain a path to upper management. The Design Release Engineer position was the steppingstone to becoming an executive at GM or Delphi.

After I started my work with Jageer, he didn't talk to me for the first three weeks. I often asked him questions, to which he simply stared at me in response, continuing his work without a word. I was roused by my co-workers who'd poke fun. Instead of complaining when they asked about my experience working with Jageer, I was determined not to give up because Jageer was not mad at me. He was upset with the establishment that did not do right by him. He was better than all those guys, and at one time, they had even worked for him. He had fallen out of favor, and they bust him down. That was his pain, and I had empathy for him.

I could have easily complained to human resources or to my boss and said I could not handle the difficult work environment. However, there was a lesson to be learned. So, I went to Jageer one day and asked him about his life. I said, "Can you tell me about your children and your culture? I want to learn more." I really did want to learn more about him. So, Jageer and I started having conversations. Every morning, before I jumped right into discussions about work, I said something like, "Jageer, let's go get a cup of coffee. I want to hear some more about how you came up, your career, and what led you here."

Those conversations were magnificent because they started a relationship where he looked after me like I was one of his children. I was probably about twenty-seven and Jageer was sixty-three years old. He walked every morning, was in great health, and looked amazing for his age. I traveled with him to the plants.

He helped me and taught me so much about the architecture of a vehicle, its wiring, electrical systems, and power distribution. He explained what specific clips were for and how to solve problems. He taught me design on the biggest scale. He also taught me how to distribute power throughout the entire vehicle, and how to appropriately size wires for the current ratings. I knew these things in theory, but I did not know them as they pertain to a vehicle. At that time, the bus electrical components (BEC) were being introduced to cars. Today, cars have wiring all over them, and this was the beginning of that technology. I was able to gain knowledge and career guidance from Jageer by becoming his friend and building a relationship with him.

That experience at Delphi taught me to not only enjoy the ride but to also build relationships along the way. Relationships are foundational to realizing your purpose. Those folks become your influences and ultimately aid you in making good decisions. Calculus and physics are important, but the people that you studied calculus and physics with are arguably even more important. Those experiences and lessons are transferred from person to person, and if you are open and willing, those hard jobs become relationally hard jobs where you get to know your colleagues and build rapport with everyone. The work will always be hard, but the relationship will get you through it. Looking back, laying bricks with my grandfather was hard, hot, sticky, and sweaty work, but the relationships I had with him, and the team motivated me to go to work each day and perform my best.

I enjoy my present-day job because I love the relationships that I build along the way to help my team solve problems. Leading integrated supply chain is hard. Global commodities are higher; we are inflated from a logistics standpoint by eight times; retaining labor is difficult and more expensive; everything is inflating; and we have unprecedented demand. Despite all this, I love it.

I look at these challenges as just part of the journey. In your life's journey, the goal is not just to get to the mountaintop. The goal is to also bring folks there with you and help folks get there before you. The goal is to share in all the wonderful things that happened with those you meet along the way. Those will be the people who put you in remembrance of what is great and joyful as you overcome difficulties. As you gain experience from the challenging work, appreciate all the wonderful people who pour into you as well as those whom you can pour into. Ultimately, that is what will sustain you and take you to your destiny.

MENTAL
CHALLENGES

Demanding work is mentally challenging and straining. It will push you to your limits and make you want to quit. Long after your body wants to give up, your mental strength is what must keep you going. Even though we are each purposed for greatness, many cannot get past the mental tests, and often fall short of the place they were destined to be.

At times, you will think that you are going crazy, and you will question whether to stay the course. That is an indicator that you are on the right path and close to accomplishing your goal, so don't quit. That also means you are learning and facing the obstacles that can make you grow. Things that are too easy do not give you the experience necessary to deal with the harder things that will come your way. One of the hardest things that you are going to have to deal with in this life is maintaining the perseverance needed to press through despite how you feel.

Mental fortitude is gained through cultivating your internal conviction and belief in yourself. The decision of whether you are a success or a failure is a function of your mindset. The determination of whether you are winning or losing at accomplishing your purpose is also made in your mind.

That battlefield of the mind is where you develop strategies to attack what attacks you. The Bible speaks about being overcome by the word of your testimony. What that means is that after you go through the test, which exists in your mind, you are an overcomer. Then, your testimony allows you to reflect on all the different things that you had to do to get through that obstacle. That is the importance of taking the challenging work.

Kobe Bryant championed the Mamba mentality, which is the discipline to win and not let your lack of persistence or mental fortitude be the biggest obstacle. The work that he put in to consistently practice long after he was tired was a function of his mentality. This type of drive and execution is only possible when you conquer the battlefield of the mind.

The battle is you against you, and that is a tough pill for a lot of people to swallow. It is easier to shun responsibility, blame other people, and give up. You must be willing to continually work very hard. That is solely dependent on you. **You** must develop strategies to deal with temporary defeat. **You** must also recognize what **you** have accomplished, how you have overcome, and what you have endured. You build mental toughness through the process of holding yourself accountable.

When assessing your current state, you must mindfully and strategically handle your present challenges. On the lonely and tiring days when you want to give up, remind yourself that these days are just part of the journey that you have signed up for. The journey to your destiny is not always easy as it has dips, rocks, mudslides, and cliffs that make you want to stop. It is not a walk in the park; it is a journey that you must mentally prepare for. This process will condition and protect your mind, then your body will follow suit.

Undoubtedly, you will have no shortage of contrarians. You must protect your mind from anyone who attempts to tell you anything that contradicts where you want to be. That may be friends, family members, pastors, leaders, or anyone who opposes what you believe you have been called and destined for. We, as humans, are wired to listen to bad things, which is unfortunate. So, you must be mentally tough enough to not allow anyone to penetrate your mind.

You must strengthen your mental toughness until negativity no longer bothers you to the point that it stalls progress. Live life expecting things to go well but prepare for when things do not. As you protect and condition your mind, you can celebrate the wonderful accomplishments on the way to your destiny.

One of my earliest moments of understanding mental toughness occurred when I was a little kid spending time with my Uncle Herbert and his family. I rode along with my Uncle Herbert and my cousin, Adria, on a trip to the bank. Uncle Herbert left my cousin and me in the car for a moment while he went in to handle his business. I was a scared little kid at times, and I just started crying and crying. He was gone for less than a minute when I rolled down the window to yell his name. He came back and said, "What are you doing? You're rolling down the window, and you're going to let somebody in here." He began to talk to me about being mindful of my emotions. He asked me why I was crying and when I responded that I was scared, he spoke about how fear can stop progress. This may have been my first lesson on mental toughness. Even as a child, I knew I wanted to continue moving forward and the thought of me stopping straightened me up.

Uncle Herbert was someone I looked up to because he had the family that I dreamed of, consisting of my three cousins, Adria, Herbert Jr., and Howard, and my Auntie Ann, who is my mom's sister. They did so many things together, and some years, I went to visit in the summer. Also, when I was young, he bought me shoes when I needed them. Uncle Herbert was always impressed with just me, and he did not know it, but I was paying attention.

We must pay attention to and get the lessons from these life experiences. A mindful person learns by observing the examples that others set and the words that they say. Lessons often do not come in a sit-down conversation where someone tells you exactly what to expect. Life reveals different things to you along the way. From Uncle Herbert, I learned about the importance of being a confident, smart, good-looking, and fearless Black man who was a dad. He was a man that provided for his family and poured into a kid that wasn't even his. In the same way that I looked at my aunts as mother figures, I looked at him as a father figure.

Sometimes, people that don't have dads and didn't grow up with the traditional family structure will remain stagnant in some areas of life. Those of us with that history can instead look for father figures as they reveal themselves to us. Sometimes, the father that you were raised with is not the person that you will want to look up to as your father figure. When that's the case, and even when it's not, there's an unsurmountable amount of knowledge that can be gained from other father figures around you.

When times get tough, you need to pull on these life lessons to help you get through. Pull on the things that people have coached you through and the examples they have set. These experiences will help you get through challenging situations where people ask you uncomfortable questions. In those instances, I pull on things that my aunts, grandparents, mom, uncles, coaches, or stepdad taught me. I had a lot of different people who gave me nuggets along the way to help me during times I question and wonder which way to go. These influences help to discern the direction.

Remember, those who wander are not always lost. Some believe in a higher power and have faith that pulls them in the right direction. To the average observer, this may look like wandering. Walking by faith often means simply following that nudge or intuition that is drawing you when you are unsure of where to go. That nudge that guides you in the right direction can be a gift you receive because of your faithfulness. That is such a wonderful thing, and it helps you during your darkest times.

One of my darkest seasons was from 2001 through 2006. As I reflect on the challenges I experienced in work and life during that time, I can testify to the power of destiny. While navigating those early milestones in my career and caring for a family, I often found myself unclear about the right steps. I relied on my faith to guide me and pull me toward the destiny that is my life manifested today. Although this season of my life took place two decades ago, that time has flown by, and it seems like yesterday. We all go through hard experiences that force us to rely on faith. Once on the other side, hopefully, we can look back and say, "That was amazing," or "I learned from that experience." As times get tough, look toward your destiny and operate in faith so that you don't resist the pull. Ultimately, as you follow the pull, you win by getting to your destiny.

I like to win, and I get great satisfaction when I state and complete my goals. Some of my goals are not completed quickly and require me to perform mental gymnastics to get them done. I work in integrated supply chain, and this has been the most difficult sector to work in for any company during the last few years. There has been unprecedented demand and lead time on components, as well as difficulties with labor and with getting products to the ports. So, I try to figure out how I can get more into my manufacturing plants so that we can build products and get them to our customers.

I solve a lot of different problems with many different variables. For a lot of those variables, I cannot formulate an equation to get to the answers. That is mentally challenging, and at times, I feel temporary defeat. It's a tough job. However, I have the forethought to understand that for every problem there is a solution. My path to finding that solution is dependent upon my ability to lean into that problem and visualize the outcome. This experience, though difficult, is a vital building that will equip me in becoming a capable CEO. These are the obstacles that are an indirect part of the job. The folks that will come up against you will be plentiful as you get closer to that destiny.

I want to introduce the term *microaggression* that comes with the mental challenges affixed to the challenging work. Historically, racial microaggressions have been a major source of mental challenges for minorities in the corporate arena. These are indirect, subtle, or unintentional acts of discrimination against members of a marginalized group. Microaggressions stop us in our tracks because they often catch us off guard. We've heard them described as death by a thousand paper cuts or be likened to an invisible knife in someone's back. It is very tough to sit in meetings and constantly be bombarded by passive-aggressive comments from individuals, which cause discord for no reason.

Often, the appropriate response, which is to call out the behavior and not allow it to persist, is not the response given. We tend to endure it in silence and feel torment. That is the toughest mental challenge you must break through, especially early in your career. We are subjected to microaggressions throughout our careers until we have the authority to do something to address it for ourselves and others.

Microaggressions are meant to stifle you and hurt you. They are designed to make you doubt yourself. Doubt is fear, which is the opposite of faith and belief. If you don't believe in your vision or expected outcome, or if you lack the confidence to accomplish that challenging job, microaggressions will feed any sense of self-doubt.

Once you start receiving those microaggressions that come along with the challenging work, you are on the right track, and you will need to press through. You will need to create a network of mentors, allies, and trusted comrades so that you discuss what you are enduring in an open and accepting environment. This is critical for your mental health. Most times, microaggressions go unnoticed by all except the person at whom they are directed, and those who may have experienced them before. This behavior is rooted in stereotypes and hate that comes from an intimidated and insecure individual. This person sees your light and knows that you are destined for great work. Their goal is to stop you.

I have had many experiences with microaggressions in Corporate America, and they continue in some form even today. Those people don't focus on the six degrees I have from top-notch institutions. Instead, they make statements like, "You dress nice," or "You speak well," or "You write well." When I make suggestions, they say things like, "We did that before. That's not going to work." They throw darts at everything I do. They exaggerate the 5% of a task that didn't go as planned and downplay the successful 95%. They are constant critics who always have something negative to say.

As you take on challenging work, these types of obstacles are expected. Years ago, I was at a company, and I had to replace an individual who worked on my team. The individual remained in the organization, and we sat in meetings together. That individual, who was mad at other folks, took it out on me with constant poking and berating. He spoke negatively about my work and said that it was not as good as people thought it was. He said that I was just a talker. There is nothing that I hate more than hearing that commentary about me because it lends to the fallacy that Black folks are bullshitters; we don't pay attention to detail; and we cannot do engineering work. He said those things in meetings, and made snippy remarks like, "Hmm, we'll see if it works." He was simply irritating.

I did not stand up and say, "Hey, sir, you are exhibiting microaggressions." I did not have anyone to talk to either. It was frustrating and stressful to endure this behavior, but I had the belief and the self-confidence to press through. I do not want you to do what I did and endure this type of attack alone. I encourage you to lean on your allies. Don't sit and take the death by a thousand paper cuts. Express your feelings in a safe space.

Microaggressions and other mental challenges will always be commonplace in a corporate environment. Therefore, we must intentionally choose a positive outlook. I choose to speak life into situations rather than death. I choose to highlight what will get resolved as opposed to what will remain unsolved. I will approach each situation from a solution-focused mindset rather than a problem-focused one. I will not simply read the news and tell people what I cannot do; I will make the news, and I will tell them what I *can* do.

Having a can-do attitude will help you fight in the battlefield of the mind. You must speak over your problem and have an internal battle with it. As you audibly declare victory over a thing, something transforms within your brain, and that is why confessions are important. Usually, if a person confesses the negative, the negative will manifest. They will get depressed and feel defeated. Out of the mind of a person, the mouth speaks. As you formulate positivity in your brain and speak life into a situation, you formulate your desired end. This is how you manifest positive outcomes.

In short, the realization of your vision happens in the battlefield of the mind. As you subdue your mind, focus on the positive outcome, which is your calling. Of course, we all have moments where we feel down, just don't stay down or defeated. As soon as you let that habit of defeatist thinking take hold, that becomes who you are. So, you go to the pit of despair and become that which you worry about and lament over. You become fearful, sad, depressed, unaccomplished, and a person no one wants to be around because nothing goes your way.

Alternatively, as you conquer the battlefield of your mind, you become more positive in your thinking and that becomes your habit. You draw people near to you and become the light. That is the beauty of getting your mind under control. In that battlefield of the mind, you must be able to recognize challenges and speak life to your circumstances. You must take your thoughts captive and cover them with your destiny and your strategic steps. You must execute to get to your vision and accomplish your purpose. Remember, the battle is you against you!

PATIENTLY
IMPATIENT

To be patiently impatient is an interesting concept. That phrase is almost counter to what we are advised to do, which is to be patient and wait. Without question, patience is a virtuous attribute to have in your arsenal, but I do not want you to assume it must be passive. Being patiently impatient means that you are actively waiting. It means that while you're waiting, you are conscious and aware of the things that are happening around you and looking for growth opportunities. It means that while you are waiting, you are learning and preparing for action, not just lamenting over losses.

As you are waiting, wait patiently, but with a sense of urgency and hustle like the rent is due. Never quit! Continue to move forward in everything that you do, even if you get knocked backward. If that happens, sit there, and ask yourself, "Why?" Ponder a bit, but then get back up and keep pressing. Be patiently impatient!

Get everything you need out of each job, but do not stay in any position longer than necessary. Once you have accomplished your goals at a certain level and have a win or even a loss, recognize that it may be time to move forward. Do not chew that gum after it has lost its flavor. Do not be content just because you have something to chew on. Spit that piece out and get another because that experience is over. Know when it is time to move on and when it is time to embark on the next journey.

Also, do not let anyone tell you that you need more time in an experience or a role. If you know beyond a shadow of a doubt that it is time for you to move on, be patiently impatient. Do not overstay your welcome. I have had jobs before where I spent time learning, with different leaders expressing that they wanted me to stay a little longer. Often, when a leader tells you that, they are doing so for their own benefit, not yours. People will try to keep you under them or next to them to do all the hard work (usually with no credit) and are not always looking out for your best interest.

With every role, you must acknowledge what you have learned and be very self-aware to understand your best career options. You must also be mindful and aware of when it is time to leave and progress to the next stage of your development.

Some people may be scared to move forward because the higher you go up that mountain towards that castle on the hill, the more difficult it becomes. The air up there is a little different. You cannot breathe as easily, and it is a little colder. There are more rocks, and the falls are steeper. It is uncharted and not many people can tell you about it. Therefore, you may want to stop more often than you did when you were closer to the bottom of the hill.

Sometimes, you may be tempted to stay too long in a situation, and veil it as patience. You might say something like, "I'm just waiting for the Lord to tell me to move." The Lord told you to move as soon as He said, "Let there be light." The Lord told you to move as soon as He blew breath into your lungs. You are veiling patience as though you are being virtuous, but it is fear of failure. You must be self-aware and able to tell yourself to move even if you don't want to.

Self-awareness is your ability to have a clear vision in the forefront of your mind. This allows you to assess whether you are marching toward your destiny. That is why the scorecard and the chronicling of your wins and losses are so important. This will keep you on track. You have a timeline and you have been purposed for something great. Don't let patience stop you. You must use your faith, which is the corresponding action to what you believe, to make strides. Vision and faith are tied at the hip. Faith, like vision, is a belief and a hope based on the unseen that you must walk toward to get to your calling!

As you move up in leadership roles, you must take those leaps of faith. As you become patiently impatient, you win. As you take those steps and conquer the battlefield of the mind, you win. As you continue to battle through those obstacles and experiences, you win. Once you start to check off all the different goals in your plan, you win. You start that momentum that you have been working hard to get going. It overtakes you and pulls you to the finish line. Your job is to not give up, but to keep moving and become patiently impatient.

There will be environments and people that you cannot control. Realize that you can only control yourself and your responses to your environment. The place you end up in is ultimately up to you. As we reflect on the advice given throughout this book, we can conclude that you are in control of your will to go forward and establish your vision. Great things are always in store for the person that walks by faith. Faith starts with an effort, a step, and is you against you. Your corresponding action will take you toward that place called destiny.

I make statements like *faith means move* and *fear means stop,* and it is just that simple. Fear has a paralyzing effect. It does not even encourage you to go backward; it just causes you to stop in your tracks. Inaction is even worse than going backward. At least if you were going backward, there would be some action, and you would be gaining more experience and maybe learning more lessons to eventually propel you forward.

If you move backward, you might revisit things from your past and gain some motivation to move forward. It may serve as a reminder that the best, like an old childhood sweater, does not fit you in anymore. It does not serve you anymore. Instead of providing warmth, it now only provides discomfort. That's the thing about fear, it will keep you where you are. Going backward may give you the motivation to take that other step. The trajectory of life takes many twists and turns, but it consistently moves in a direction. Never let fear make you stop moving toward your destiny.

Muhammad Ali had a great vision statement, which was also a confession. He said, "I am the greatest because I said I am the greatest." He professed to be the greatest. So, when I think of him saying, "Rumble young man, rumble. I shook up the world," I am reminded that rumbling is an action. It involves tearing through things, making things uncomfortable, and being disruptive. As you pursue your purpose, you will make yourself and others uncomfortable. However, you will do so to fulfill your purpose to get to your destiny.

Think back to all the adversity you have faced throughout your life that you have kept rumbling through. You have made it this far, so keep on rumbling. If someone comes against you and says, "You can't do this! This has not been done this way before," then rumble and keep going. When you get to a fork in the road and you don't know which way to go, don't stop. Use your best judgment and pick a direction. If it gets you to what turns out to be the wrong place, burst through that mountain that is next to it, and get on that other path.

Oftentimes, we stop at the fork in the road, and we are scared to rumble or to disrupt. Don't be afraid. Know that you are the greatest and declare that you are the greatest. You are here to make an impact that the world has never seen before. You must keep disrupting and learning from uncommon things.

Get comfortable with the uncomfortable. Whenever I think about something rumbling or shaking, I think of an earthquake. Isn't an earthquake uncomfortable? During an earthquake, the ground is unsteady, things are moving and getting out of sorts. It is shaking up what is known and the status quo. It is a shock; sometimes things must be shocked and disrupted. To progress to the next phase in your life, sometimes you must rumble.

In the Garden of Gethsemane, as Jesus pressed out His anointing, He knew that He was preparing to do work He was not ready for. *Gethsemane* means "oil press," and to get olive oil, you must press that olive so much just to get a small yield. Olive oil is used for anointing, which is a purpose or destiny. Jesus was going to be the Savior of the world, but He was going to have to die to do it. That was His next appointment. He had to rumble it, shake it, stir it, press it, and be uncomfortable with it. He cried and lamented, yet He still did it to fulfill His purpose and accomplish His calling!

I need you to press through, just like Jesus did. Know that even though it is hard, and you don't want to do it, you must rumble young person rumble. Feel the weight of the challenge. Shake your head and say you're not going to do it. Yell and lament about it. Then, take that step, because once you take that first step, on faith that second step is easier. Rumble young person rumble. The first step is often the hardest, but it is the most necessary to get you to your destiny.

I wish I could tell you that it will be easy, but it will not. Sometimes, we do things in this life for the people coming after us who are meant to be great. Sometimes, we must be the trailblazers who open space for everyone else to have a seat at the table. We must shock the world in every aspect of our lives so that we can continually move forward. Sometimes, people die before they see their vision unfold. Ask Dr. King and Malcolm X about that. They knew their vision and purpose, and they knew what they had to do to fulfill it. They also knew the potentially catastrophic end. Yet, they still did it. Rumble young person rumble. Press forward. Fulfill your purpose. Get your divine appointment and step in faith.

Those big dreams we had as children let us know that we were born to be great. Be great and take this world by storm. With storms come rain, wind, and change. In life, when storms come, some things are blown away, some seeds are nurtured, and some things are flooded or washed away. Ultimately, storms shock the system, and I desire for you to shock the system and get to your destiny.

Let's reflect upon the global pandemic that started in 2020. At that time, we all experienced a growth in patience, and we didn't know what to do. We had no idea what sitting at home and being isolated meant. We had to spend a lot of time being patiently impatient. We had to explore new ways to get groceries and other essential items we took for granted because we did not know how long the pandemic would last. We had no idea when we would see or talk to our co-workers or loved ones in person again. We wondered if we would ever be able to engage with other people without masks.

During the pandemic, working in the plant without the option for my employees or me to work from home was very challenging. As an operations leader, I could have easily looked at the world as though it were coming to an end, but I chose to have a positive outlook for the future. I chose to believe that things would change, and that we would be able to see each other's smiling faces and work without masks again someday. This eventually came true!

Working in integrated supply chain, supply chain, or operations during a worldwide pandemic has not been for the weak at heart. In 2016 or 2017, supply chain management degrees were very popular, and a lot of sexy jobs were available to the masses. Many people went back to school to earn MBAs with supply chain management specialization. Then, the pandemic hit, and we all came to realize who was truly dedicated to this work. It became too hard, required too many hours, and a lot of people left the field (they did not want that smoke!).

During the height of the pandemic, we questioned how to manage supply continuity and how to manage people working from home so that we could build products in our manufacturing sites. Supply was down, and we did not have the capacity we needed to build the demand because we lacked labor. We had to become creative and manifest what we wanted in this situation by being positive and patiently impatient.

At the start of the pandemic, I worked at Carrier Corporation, and I spent a lot of long hours figuring out the best practices in supply chain. I do the same now at the Toro Company. I must determine the best way to work with suppliers, make sure folks are safe in our plants, and ensure that we can build what our customers want so they can function. In this current market, the constraint to our company's top-line revenues and bottom-line earnings is in the hands of the supply chain and how we manage issues.

We constantly hear about how critical supply chain is to our bottom line from Wall Street news, urgent investment calls, and earnings releases. The success of a company's supply chain will determine whether that company succeeds or fails in the marketplace. Supply chain is hard and challenging work. It is fulfilling work, but it can take a toll on you both mentally and physically. I have always been the one to run towards the fire because I know that there is a reward on the other side. I know that when you run towards the fire, you learn things about yourself that you didn't know. Fire is a great purifier and a way to figure out what you are made of. If you truly want to accelerate your career and jump over your peers, run towards the fire.

Supply chain during the pandemic these past three years has been that fire experience. During this time, I have gained major growth in the critical leadership skills I need for my career trajectory. When asked why I didn't go to another part of the business, such as sales or marketing, I respond that it has been my opportunity to embrace the challenging work. I know when I pick the challenging work, it will pay dividends on the other side. The skills that I have added to my toolkit over the past three years have accelerated my progress in becoming a stronger business leader and ultimately a CEO.

Within supply chain, I have had opportunities to stretch my brain as I have contemplated complex business problems. I am happy to be the person that the company looks toward to ensure that we reach our quarterly and yearly revenue goals. Executives need to accept this challenging work to be prepared. The root word of *executive* is *execute*, and the challenging work will always require you to execute it.

It is predicted that in the future, most CEOs will be picked from those who ran the supply chain organizations. Contrast this to the 1980s when CEOs were picked from sales organizations, the 1990s and 2000s when they were picked from finance units, and the 2010s when they were picked from information technology sectors. On the other side of this supply chain crisis, CEOs will be picked from folks who managed complexities and ensured companies were sustainable.

Eventually, some companies did not make it through this crisis. For the successful ones, I promise you that they had someone who was very strong and dedicated to the supply chain organization and leaned into the challenging work.

Now, I will give you an example of these leadership strategies put together. During the pandemic, I transitioned into leading the Residential and Light Commercial Systems (RLCS) at the Carrier Company. I resided in Florida at the time, and the biggest plant in Carrier was in Collierville, Tennessee. RCLS was based in Indianapolis, so I bought a townhome there. The work that needed to be done to produce more in Carrier's RCLS division specifically was in that plant in Collierville, right outside Memphis.

In Collierville, they build split systems, which are air conditioning units that also have heat pumps and can produce heat. We had to produce almost 30% more units because we had an unprecedented backlog. People were at home more, so they were using their air conditioners more, and we were taking share based on how much we could produce in the factories. So, instead of trying to lead from Indianapolis, I decided to temporarily move to Tennessee before I even stayed in my townhome in Indianapolis. I stayed in hotels at first, then in a company apartment so that I could be hands-on with my senior director, Steven Youngblood, in Collierville. I wanted to be there to understand the constraints that were stopping us from producing more. I had to take on the challenging work, accept the mental obstacles, and be patiently impatient to achieve my vision of getting us more products to service our customer demand.

In Collierville, initially, we questioned whether the cause of why we could not provide more for our customers was labor. We had an attrition issue, which pointed to the culture, so we had to work on strengthening the culture by leaning into employee engagement. We looked at supply, which was highly constrained. We purchased aluminum and copper, which were constrained because labor was constrained across the supply chain due to the pandemic. People were at home and scared, not knowing when the madness would end. After analysis, changeovers ended up being the root cause of why we could not run efficiently. We would rob ourselves of the necessary throughput to make our backlog. Even though the analysis showed that result, it became important to understand the true capacity of that plant. I would not have been able to identify that and help change the trajectory of the plant if I had sat in my office and tried to lead from Indianapolis at home. I needed to be right on the floor to understand, coach, and help.

The twelve-hour days in steel-toed boots were hard. I had to take off my business suits and put on my khakis again; I had to go from the top floor to the plant floor. I had to walk around with my high-traffic vest and mask on all day. Sometimes, I had to go in during the evening shift just to see how we could push through and get units out. I had to use my strategies to work this difficult job. I had to be patiently impatient to bring my vision of increasing productivity at the

Collierville plant to pass. Although it was difficult, it was also rewarding. We made the company billions of dollars, and we had a record year. I still had five other plants to lead, but I led them from the plant that had the most issues and required me to be there with them. I could have easily pointed fingers or sat back, but I decided to attack. I decided to accept the challenging work, and it unlocked a part of my skill set that I had not polished as well. I knew it in theory, and I had in-depth knowledge of operations leadership or leading a plant because I worked on different sides of it, but I never had true ownership of a plant of that magnitude.

During that season, I was able to understand the ins and outs of working on a manufacturing floor. This unique experience gave me knowledge of every lever one could pull in integrated supply chain. I dealt with manufacturing engineering, quality, design engineering, program management, new product development, automation deployment, manufacturing strategies, capacity analysis, and other ancillary sectors. Before this experience, I had never been right on the floor of a manufacturing plant of this magnitude for day-to-day operations. Serving on this scale has equipped me to assess issues in a plant quickly and to understand the constraints so that we can improve throughput, which is to simply get more products to customers.

This plant experience helped me develop my overarching strategy of transformation for integrated supply chain, which includes safety, throughput, and cultural transformation. In supply chain, we must keep employees safe, and we must produce more by identifying constraints. The foundation of an organization must be built upon everyone embracing that we are a culture of one. That is what transforms an organization. I am grateful for the hands-on experience I gained in Collierville supporting some of the best men and women to help Carrier become successful. Those were hot and tiring days. My brain was fatigued, yet I had to go on, and I am better for it.

There will come a time when you will be consumed with what you see, and it will seem as though you are stagnant. Reflect upon the 2020 pandemic, then think about where you are now. The pandemic changed the world because it made us pause, take stock, and appreciate life. Reflecting upon challenges helps you ideate a better tomorrow. Being patiently impatient is all about walking towards your hope for tomorrow in every action that you take today.

Despite the pandemic, I was patiently impatient by not only excelling in my role at Carrier Corporation, but also by transferring from Carrier to another promotion at The Toro Company as an executive officer in the supply chain seat. If I had adopted the belief that things would always be that way, I would not have thought past what I saw. I encourage you to think past what is right in front of you and hold tight to your faith in what can happen.

Epilogue

As we conclude, I hope that the tips shared in this guide will always inspire you to move in the direction of your destiny, fueled and filled by faith. I hope that these tips empower you to relentlessly pursue your purpose. That, my friend, is why I provided these action statements. Vision challenging work, mental strength, and being patiently impatient are all about action. They are steps along the journey that will get you to your destiny!

You must have unwavering faith that no matter what happens, you will accomplish that which you were purposed for. Remember that the definition of faith is the corresponding action to what you believe. You must walk confidently, even in the face of downright dirty people. Let your light shine, but never forget that not all people like the light. Some people prefer darkness because it allows them to sneak around and be negative.

Each one of us was made to do something great. We were not made by happenstance or to wander around aimlessly. We were made for a purpose, and someone is depending on you to find that purpose.

Hopefully, this book has blessed you as much as it has blessed me to write it. Be confident, faithful, diligent, tough, unwavering, relentless, and resilient to push through any and every obstacle that is put before you. If you can't go around, go under. If you can't go under, go through. If you can't go through, jump over it. No matter what, get around it. Realize what you were purposed to do and be ready to shock the system and take the world by storm. I'll see you at the top of the hill.

So do not fear, for I am with you, do not be dismayed for I am your God. I will strengthen you and help you; I will uphold you with my righteous, right hand.

Isaiah 41:10

About the Author

Kevin is the Chief Supply Chain Officer for The Toro Company. In his role, he has responsibility for procurement, manufacturing, order services, transportation, safety, quality, service, and productivity for products that generate approximately $5 billion of revenue.

He previously served as Vice President of Operations for Residential and Light Commercial Systems at Carrier and held other leadership positions in the organization including Vice President of Quality and Continuous Improvement and Vice President of Advanced Manufacturing. Prior to joining Carrier, Carpenter was Vice President of Manufacturing Services at Rockwell Automation, Inc. He also held earlier Engineering and Operations roles at General Electric, Magna International, Nexxus Lighting and General Motors/Delphi.

Kevin has a proven track record of outstanding leadership and operational expertise. He has transformed organizations to enable companies to experience revenue and earnings growth by driving operational excellence in the integrated supply chain. Kevin is presently a board member of the Engineering

Dual Degree/AUC Atlanta University Consortium, and a former board member of the Urban League Cleveland (2016-2019). He has also recently received notable awards and recognition as a 2022 Most Influential Black Executive by Savoy Magazine, and recipient of the 2022 Supply Chains to Admire.

For over two decades, Kevin has provided inclusive access through mentorship and internship opportunities to students of the Atlanta University Center Consortium, National Society of Black Engineers, and the National Black MBA Association to name a few. He has provided approximately $3M in corporate support to fund students' ability to attend conferences, job fairs, and professional development training.

Kevin holds a Master of Business Administration from the Weatherhead School of Management at Case Western Reserve, a Master of Science in Industrial Engineering and Engineering Management from Youngstown State University, a Bachelor of Science in Electrical Engineering from Georgia Institute of Technology and a Bachelor of Science in General Engineering, with a Minor in Mathematics, from Morehouse College. He also completed Finance for Senior Executives at Harvard Business School in 2021, holds a Master of Arts in Biblical Studies from Ashland University, and two design patents in the Electrical industry.

Made in United States
Orlando, FL
04 August 2023